TUTANKHA

AND THE GOLDEN AGE OF THE PHARAOHS

Alex Yates

A SOUVENIR BOOK

ZAHI HAWASS

PHOTOGRAPHS BY KENNETH GARRETT

NATIONAL GEOGRAPHIC

Washington, D.C.

TUTANKHAMUN RETURNS

Since the discovery of his tomb in 1922, Tutankhamun has fascinated the world. His name alone conjures up images of glittering gold and gleaming jewels, of riches beyond the imagination, and of a life cut tragically short. His treasures have attracted millions of visitors, both to their permanent home in Cairo and to traveling exhibitions that have circled the globe.

Only about eight or nine years old when he came to the throne in about 1332 B.C., Tutankhamun was heir to an immense realm that stretched north almost to the Euphrates River and south to the Fourth Cataract of the Nile. The kings who came

Inside Tutankhamun's Burial Chamber in 1925, pioneering archaeologist Howard Carter carefully cleans off the boy king's inner wooden coffin.

before him had fought to build an empire, conquering the lands to the south and forcing the city-states to the north into vassaldom. The booty they brought back poured into the royal coffers and the treasure houses of the principal state god, Amun. Tutankhamun's putative grandfather, Amenhotep III, inherited a stable kingdom and access to unmatched wealth.

But this moment of calm was not to last. Two decades before Tutankhamun ascended the throne, a new player stepped onto the stage of Egyptian history. Eldest surviving son of Amenhotep III and his great queen Tiye, the "heretic" pharaoh Akhenaten and his wife Nefertiti changed the state religion of Egypt, closing the temples of the great state gods and dedicating their extensive holdings to the sun-disk

3

Aten. Some see this controversial king as a saint, others as a monster. Many scholars believe that Tutankhamun was his son.

Soon after he became pharaoh, Tutankhamun rejected the teachings of Akhenaten, bringing back the traditional religion and restoring the wealth and power of Amun. When he died after fewer than ten years on the throne, he was laid to rest in a small tomb in the Valley of the Kings, a remote canyon on the west bank of the Nile in Thebes. Tutankhamun passed away without an heir, as did his elderly successor, Aye. Perhaps because of his association with the hated Akhenaten, the next kings wiped his name from the annals of history. Little did they know that by erasing his existence from official records, they would be ensuring that his name would live forever: While all of the later royal tombs were robbed and their treasures scattered, Tutankhamun's remained untouched, hidden safely beneath the sands.

On November 4, 1922, English archaeologist Howard Carter found the long-forgotten burial, a discovery that fired the imagination of the public. For the next decade, the world watched in amazement as thousands of objects of gold, alabaster, semiprecious stone, precious wood, and glass—each piece more astonishing than the last—poured from the tomb's packed chambers and traveled to their permanent home at the Cairo Museum.

In 1961, some of Tutankhamun's treasures left Egypt for the first time. Other traveling exhibitions followed: Between 1961 and 1981, thousands of people stood in line for hours to catch a glimpse of these riches as they were displayed around the world. In the late 1970s, a special exhibition of 50 of the best objects from the tomb launched a frenzy of Tutmania.

Two decades ago, a statue of the goddess Selket that once guarded Tutankhamun's canopic chest was damaged while traveling in Germany. As a result of this accident as well as an increasing awareness of the unavoidable wear and tear of travel on objects, the Egyptian Parliament requested that the treasures of the king not leave the country again. This ban held for over 20 years, denying an entire generation (at least those not fortunate enough to come to Egypt) the opportunity to see artifacts from Tutankhamun's tomb.

In 2002 representatives of the Antikenmuseum, Basel, approached Egypt's

Supreme Council of Antiquities and proposed a new traveling exhibition featuring the treasures of Tutankhamun. Due in large part to the excellent relationship that Switzerland and Egypt enjoy, the Parliament agreed to allow a carefully chosen selection of pieces to travel, so that the world could once again experience the wonders of the boy king firsthand.

Tutankhamun's treasures are not traveling alone; with them come objects spanning a century of Egyptian history. Most are from the burial ground of the pharaohs—the Valley of the Kings. There are pieces from the tombs of Amenhotep II and his son, Tuthmosis IV; from the burial of Amenhotep III's parents-in-law, Yuya and Tjuya, and from the mysterious Tomb 55, which may have held the body of Akhenaten himself. The exhibition also showcases objects from the temples on the east bank at Thebes (across the river from the royal valley) and from Akhenaten's capital city, Tell el Amarna. These pieces illuminate the world into which the boy king was born and tell the story of the Golden Age of Egypt, when the Egyptian empire was at its height and gold flowed like dust in the land of the pharaohs.

Found with hundreds of other shabtis in Tutankhamun's tomb, this elegant limestone statuette of the king bore the inscription: "The good god, Lord of the Two Lands, Nebkheprure, beloved of Osiris, the great god."

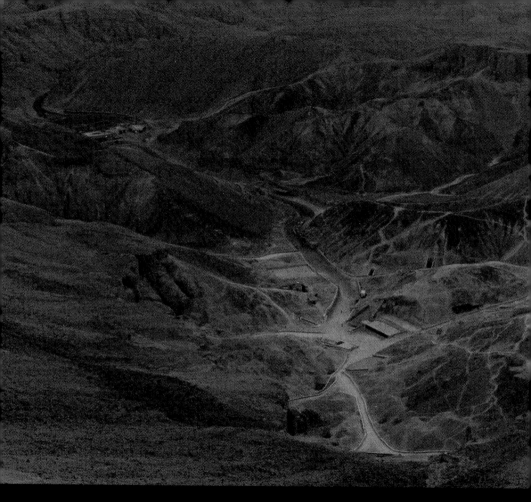

18th DYNASTY

| 3000 | | 2500 | | 2000 | | 1500 |

Late Predynastic
circa 3100 B.C.

Early Dynastic
ca 2950–2575 B.C.

Old Kingdom
ca 2575–2150 B.C.

1st Intermediate
Period
ca 2125–1975 B.C.

Middle Kingdom
ca 1975–1640 B.C.

2nd Intermediate
Period
ca 1630–1520 B.C.

Against the backdrop of the Valley of the Kings, a timeline of ancient Egypt's dynasties spans more than 3,000 years.

	1000		500		A.D.

THE 18TH DYNASTY

The pharaonic civilization to which Tutankhamun was heir first appears in the historical record in about 3150 B.C., near the end of what Egyptologists call the Predynastic Period. By about 2950 B.C., all of Egypt had been brought under the control of a single king. From this point forward, modern scholars divide the history of Egypt into periods and dynasties, based on a system laid out by the Greek-Egyptian priest Manetho in the 3rd century B.C.

Tutankhamun was born into the 18th dynasty, founded c. 1539 B.C. by its first ruler, Ahmosis. Ahmosis set the pattern for the kings who came after him by acting as both war leader and builder. With Ahmosis-Nefertari, his sister-wife, he left monuments at sites including Avaris, Abydos (mythical birthplace of the god Osiris),

and Karnak, where the 18th-dynasty kings expanded the Middle Kingdom temple to Amun. Although Thebes (or Waset, as it was known in ancient times) became the religious center of the country, the 18th-dynasty rulers moved their political seat to the Memphite region.

Amenhotep I, son of Ahmosis and Ahmosis-Nefertari, ruled for about 20 years and continued to build the empire for which his father had planted the seeds. His successful Nubian wars replenished the kingdom's coffers, and he opened a number of quarries and mines to provide material for his many building projects. These included a chapel at Karnak, bark stations— places where the sacred boats of the gods could rest during their festival journeys— on the west bank of Thebes, and monuments at Abydos as well as in the region of the First Cataract of the Nile, the southern border of Egypt proper.

Amenhotep I does not seem to have left behind any sons. The next king, thought by some to have been from a family connected with the priesthood of Amun, was Tuthmosis I. Tuthmosis I ruled for about 11 years, campaigning vigorously for much of his reign. It is likely that he was responsible for the extension of the southern border of Egypt to somewhere between the Second and Third Cataracts.

Tuthmosis I was the first in a line of Tuthmosids, powerful kings and queens who eventually brought the Egyptian empire to its farthest extent, from the Fourth Cataract of the Nile in the south to the Euphrates River in the north.

This era of wealth and stability would soon by tested by the dynasty's maverick pharaoh, Amenhotep IV (later known as Akhenaten). From the beginning of his reign, Amenhotep IV is linked with his Great Royal Wife, Nefertiti—The Beautiful One Comes—who played an important role in his court. Amenhotep IV and Nefertiti had six daughters together, but apparently no sons. Another of his wives, Kiya, was

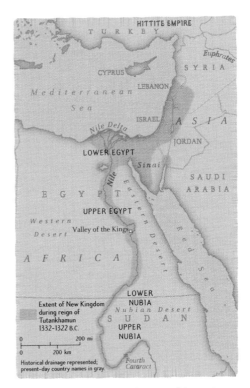

A map of ancient Egypt shows the extent of the empire during the reign of Tutankhamun.

given the special title, "Greatly Beloved Wife of the King"; she may have been Tutankhamun's mother.

In his early years of rule, the king undertook an ambitious building program at Karnak, but the temples he erected were not for Amun, but were rather dedicated to a deity manifested as the disk of the sun, the Aten. The artistic style seen in these temples and in other monuments from this period is unique in the history of Egyptian art. In contrast to the idealized, youthful images of the king seen in traditional Egyptian art, Amenhotep IV had himself represented in an exaggerated fashion, with a long, narrow face, prominent chin, high cheekbones, a long neck, narrow shoulders, pronounced breasts, wide hips, a sagging belly, and spindly arms and legs.

Debate has raged for decades on the reason the king and, by extension, members of the royal family and the elite chose to be shown in this fashion. Some believe that this new style was a reflection of the king's actual appearance. Others think that

This life-size granite statue of Tuthmosis IV and his mother Tiaa was buried just below the surface of the Temple of Amun at Karnak.

the king's features and body shape reflect his religious beliefs, and represent a desire to mirror the androgynous nature of his principal god, the sun disk, to whom the "Great Hymn to the Aten" (composed by the king himself) attributes the roles of both mother and father.

At some point between the fifth and seventh years of his rule, Amenhotep IV, "Amun is Satisfied," changed his name to Akhenaten, "The Transfigured Spirit of the Aten." Akhenaten transformed his supreme deity, the Aten, into the sole creator god from whom everything issued. As part of his spiritual revolution, Akhenaten abandoned Thebes as Egypt's religious center and built a new city—Akhetaten, the "Horizon of the Aten," better known by its modern name of el Amarna, or Amarna—dedicated to the cult of the Aten.

Akhenaten died after 17 years of rule. Exactly what happened toward the end of his reign is a matter of debate. At least one other pharaoh (identified by some as Nefertiti herself) ruled alongside him, and may have succeeded him briefly. But by the second or third year after his death, the throne of Egypt had passed into the untried hands of a young boy named Tutankhaten.

Two shabtis (funerary figurines) of Tjuya's husband Yuya stand in front of brightly painted shabti boxes. A number of such shabtis and shabti boxes were found in Yuya and Tjuya's tomb.

A masterpiece of the jeweler's art, this gilded funerary mask of Lady Tjuya, Amen-hotep III's mother-in-law, was intended to preserve and echo her features for eternity.

OPPOSITE: The head of a colossal statue of Amenhotep IV (Akhenaten) has the long, exaggerated features seen in the early Amarna period.

ABOVE: Found in the debris of the Great Palace at Amarna, this relief from a balustrade depicts Akhenaten, Nefertiti, and their oldest daughter making offerings to the Aten.

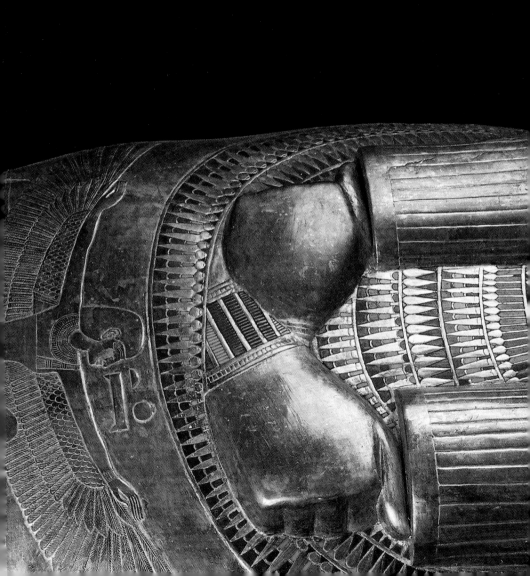

Remarkable for its serene beauty, the gilded coffin of Lady Tjuya had been opened by robbers and its contents rifled in antiquity.

OPPOSITE: This brown quartzite face of Nefertiti might have been part of a composite statue set up at Memphis.

ABOVE: A sculptor's practice model in sunk relief shows Nefertiti in the high cylindrical crown worn only by her.

OPPOSITE: The sculpted head of a princess from Amarna—one of the six daughters of Akhenaten and Nefertiti—has the elongated shape characteristic of the royal family.

ABOVE: A calcite canopic jar found in Tomb 55 in the Valley of the Kings is believed to represent Queen Kiya, one of Akhenaten's wives.

A life-size granite statue of Tutankhamun
found in the Temple of Amun at Karnak
shows the young king in a calm and
determined posture.

A knotted rope, with its necropolis seal intact, secured the doors to the second of four nested shrines in Tutankhamun's Burial Chamber.

THE LIFE AND DEATH OF TUTANKHAMUN

Young Tutankhamun would have grown up with the royal family at Amarna. He was married either before gaining the throne or very early in his reign to the third of Nefertiti and Akhenaten's six daughters, Ankhsenpaaten. A number of objects from Tutankhamun's tomb bear the queen's name alongside the king's, and others are decorated with scenes of intimacy between husband and wife, similar in style and iconography to images from Amarna but otherwise novel in Egyptian royal art. Along with their ritual meanings, these scenes may provide evidence for real affection, even love, between the royal pair.

Sometime soon after Akhenaten's passing, Tutankhaten ascended the throne of Egypt. His coronation would have been a great affair, full of pomp and pageantry.

Surrounded by courtiers and high officials, the young king would have been presented with a child-sized crook and flail, representing the power and responsibility of his new office. The priests presumably would have set on his head the crowns of Egypt, including the low red crown for Lower Egypt and the high white crown for Upper Egypt, the blue crown, the khat headdress, and the striped nemes headcloth. His brow would have been protected by the hooding cobra, Wadjet of the north, and by the vulture, Nekhbet of the south. Once the celebrations were complete, the boy was officially ruler of an empire that stretched across much of the known world.

Early in his reign, Tutankhaten began to move away from the Amarna religion, back to orthodox belief in Amun-Re and his pantheon. By his second year, the king and his queen had changed their names to Tutankhamun and Ankhsenamun, and the Amun temples at Thebes had been reopened. His artisans began to restore the name of the old god where it had been hacked out by Akhenaten's minions. Many statues and reliefs were carved for Amun's glory—with representations of the deity and his consort bearing the faces of the boy king and his young queen—and Amun's priests regained much of their former power.

Since he was still a child, Tutankhamun was particularly dependent on his advisors. The man closest to him seems to have been the "deputy of the king in the entire land," Horemheb, "Horus is in Festival". This powerful man was also Commander in Chief of the army and Overseer of All Works. Another key figure was an elderly man named Aye, who was fanbearer on the right hand of the King and Commander of the Horses. Thought by some to have been Queen Tiye's brother, and perhaps also Nefertiti's father, he held the ambiguous title of God's Father, which is thought perhaps to refer to royal fathers-in-law.

Tutankhamun was the last of a line founded by warrior pharaohs. The empire built by the early Tuthmosids had enjoyed stability and relative peace under Tuthmosis IV and at least part of the reign of Amenhotep III, but during the reign of Akhenaten the situation in the Near East changed dramatically. Letters from the time are full of references to chaos and turmoil, and reflect changing balances of power. In them, brother kings beg for alliances and gold, and vassal kings plead with the Egyptian pharaoh for protection from their neighbors.

Wall scenes in the tomb of General Horemheb at Saqqara hint at military conflict during the reign of Tutankhamun with the three principal enemies of the Egyptians: the Nubians, the Hittites, and the Libyans. Traditionally the pharaoh would have led the army himself, but most scholars are undecided (if the events are even real) about whether Tutankhamun marched himself or if Horemheb went in his stead. However, fragmentary battle scenes from Thebes suggest that the young king did in fact fight at least one major battle and led the Egyptian troops into battle himself.

Whether or not he actually went into battle, Tutankhamun was trained from youth to be a warrior. Six chariots were found in his tomb, at least one of which was a lightweight training or hunting vehicle. The New Kingdom pharaoh's weapon of choice was the bow, and Tutankhamun was buried with nearly 50 of various types and sizes, several of them child-sized, as well as arrows, slingshots, throwsticks, and other weapons.

Although his tomb equipment certainly indicates that military prowess was one of his major concerns, some scholars have suggested that he was not physically strong. Regardless of the reality, the message, echoed time and time again by the objects in the tomb, was that the king was victorious over all enemies.

As king of Egypt, lord of the Two Lands, Tutankhamun was also high priest of all the gods. He fashioned images of Amun, Ptah, and the other gods out of electrum and semiprecious stones, rebuilt and endowed their temples, and made offerings, paying for it all out of the royal treasury. Although much of his work was usurped or built over by later kings, monuments from his reign have been found at Karnak and Luxor; at Memphis and its necropolis, Saqqarap; and in Nubia. A significant

number of stone statues with the face of the young king—both as himself and in the guise of various deities—have survived the millennia, most from Thebes.

The king passed away without an heir. Two fetuses—one miscarried at about five months gestation and the other probably stillborn—were carefully buried with him in his tomb. These have been identified as female; most scholars believe that they were his daughters with Ankhsenamun. The royal couple had no living children.

A tomb had been started for Tutankhamun in the West Valley, near that of Amenhotep III. But he was not buried there—instead, Aye finished this large and clearly royal tomb during his short reign as pharaoh and used it for his own burial. Tutankhamun was interred in a small tomb in the royal valley. The objects from this tomb illuminate his life and inform us about his various roles as head of state, commander in chief of the army, and high priest of the gods.

A cutaway illustration shows Tutankhamun's Burial Chamber between the Antechamber and Treasury.

OPPOSITE: Two gilded wood figures from the Treasury of Tutankhamun's tomb show the king wearing the crowns of Upper and Lower Egypt.

ABOVE: This mirror case, shaped like an ankh, the hieroglyph for "life," was empty when found by excavators. Within its loop is Tutankhamun's throne name, Nebkheprure.

Two fundamental items of royal regalia, the crook and flail here were found in the Treasury of Tutankhamun's tomb.

OPPOSITE: Six chairs were found in Tutankhamun's tomb. This one, discovered in the Antechamber, is small enough for a child.

OPPOSITE: This shrine, made of wood covered with gold foil, was found in the Antechamber of Tutankhamun's tomb. The pillar inside it may once have held a statue.

ABOVE: When it was first found in Tutankhamun's tomb, this fan depicting the king in an ostrich hunt was topped by ostrich plumes.

Set into the center of the pectoral of gold inlaid with semiprecious stones and glass is Tutankhamun's "heart" scarab of green feldspar.

OPPOSITE: A ceremonial shield from Tutankhamun's tomb depicts the king as a winged sphinx standing upon the prostrate figures of his Nubian enemies.

LEFT: A silver and wood staff bearing the figure of the king as an old man may have been carried during a ritual such as a coronation or funeral ceremony.

Quite a few cosmetic items were found in
Tutankhamun's tomb, including this container
in the shape of a trussed duck or goose.

A winged cobra figure from the reign of
Amenhotep II likely represents the goddess
Meretseger, protectress of the king.

An elaborate royal diadem found on
Tutankhamun's head was designed to hold a
vulture and uraeus (cobra), icons that protected the king during life and after death.

OPPOSITE: Discovered in the Treasury, this gilded wood figure represents the god Ptah, tutelary god of Memphis and patron of artisans.

ABOVE: Also found in the Treasury was a gilded wood statue of the god Duamutef, one of the four sons of Horus responsible for protecting the body and viscera.

This miniature coffin of beaten gold from Tutankhamun's tomb held a mummified bundle of the king's viscera.

OPPOSITE: This painted calcite head was one of four stoppers
for a canopic chest found in Tutankhamun's tomb. It was
probably made for one of the kings who preceded him.

ABOVE: A cosmetic jar with a recumbent lion on its lid still
held traces of its original contents, a mixture of animal fat
and vegetable resins, when found in the Burial Chamber.

Images of Tutankhamun with various gods look on as the first all-Egyptian research team removes the lid from the outermost coffin of the world's most famous mummy.

THE MUMMY RE-EXAMINED

Before 2005, Tutankhamun's mummy had been examined only three times. In 1925, Carter's team removed it with great difficulty from its coffin, to which it was glued fast by hardened resins, cutting it into pieces in the process. Carter's scientists concluded that the king had died between the ages of 18 and 22. An English team that X-rayed the mummy in 1968 agreed with this conclusion. They also noted in the X-rays a cloudy area on the back of the skull, which they suggested was evidence that the king had been murdered by a blow to the back of the head. In addition, they found that Tutankhamun's ribs and sternum were missing. An American team X-rayed the skull again in 1978, and suggested that the king had been in his mid-twenties when he died.

I am currently the head of the Egyptian Mummy Project, designed to inventory and analyze all of the known mummies in Egypt. For this project, National Geographic Society and Siemens, Ltd., have donated to the Supreme Council of Antiquities a state-of-the-art CT scanning machine. The CT scanner takes hundreds of "slices," images of individual sections of the body, without having to move it. These slices can be taken at multiple angles, and then put all together into a complete, three-dimensional image of the body. As part of the Mummy Project, we decided to scan Tutankhamun. The mummy is in such delicate condition that we decided not to move it, but to do the examination in the Valley of the Kings.

We chose January 5, 2005 as the day for the scan. My team was completely Egyptian, and operating the machine was Egyptian technician Dr. Hani Abdel Rahman.

After the glass cover from the sarcophagus and the lid of the outermost coffin had been carefully removed, I reached inside gingerly and lifted the cotton blanket that covered Tutankhamun's face. My first impression was that he looked older than I had expected. The team moved the mummy, still in the wooden box full of sand in which Carter had left it, slowly out of the coffin and sarcophagus. I could see clearly that it was in pieces, some of which lay in the sand like stones. We continued out of the tomb, carrying the mummy to the trailer containing the CT machine. When we left the Valley of the Kings, we took with us 1,700 images, stored on the scanner's computer.

An Egyptian team, under the auspices of the Cairo University Faculty of Medicine, spent January and February analyzing the images. Their analysis confirms or clarifies many of the conclusions reached by the earlier investigators, and adds some fascinating new details. Guided by modern developmental milestones, the team has fixed the king's age at death at about 19. This is based primarily on examination of the epiphyses (the ends of the long bones),

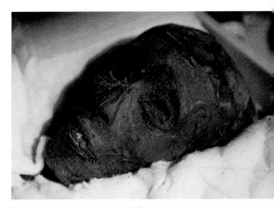

The young king's narrow, scarred face gazes across the centuries.

and confirmed by the incompletely erupted wisdom teeth. The king's overall health was good, at least to judge from his bones. He was moderately tall, perhaps about 170 cm (five and a half feet), and slightly built. He shows no signs of malnutrition or infectious disease in childhood, and seems to have been well fed and cared for. Sharing the overbite of his Tuthmosid ancestors, he had large front incisors and slightly misaligned lower teeth. The king also had a slight cleft in his hard palate. The team believes, however, that this was not severe enough to have produced a visible harelip. The young king has an extremely elongated skull, something that has been noted before but is particularly evident in the CT scan. His cranial sutures have not prematurely fused, however, allowing the team to rule out a pathological cause for this feature. Instead, they categorize this as a normal anthropological variation, one clearly depicted in Amarna art.

Tutankhamun was not murdered by a blow to the skull. There is no evidence for a partially healed injury to the back of the head, and the current team reiterates that loose pieces of bone in the skull (noted first in the 1968 X-ray) could not have come from an antemortem injury. Although part of the team believes it possible that these bones were broken by Carter's team, they think it equally plausible that the embalmers broke them while preparing the way for embalming material.

One of the most interesting theories to emerge from the analysis is that the king might have suffered an accident in which he broke his leg shortly before he died. He has a fracture of the lower left femur, at the level of the epiphyseal plate. There are many other fractures of the limbs, mostly caused by the rough handling of Carter's team, but this one is different because it has ragged rather than sharp edges, and because two thin layers of embalming fluid have entered the fracture. The majority of the team believes that this fracture must have occurred either during the embalming or, more likely, during the king's life.

The scientists note that this type of fracture is seen in young men in their late teens. If the leg was broken during life, it would have occurred a few days at the most before the king's death, as there is no evidence of extensive healing, and the associated skin wound cannot have had time to mend. Although the theorized break would not itself have been life threatening, infection might have set in. There are several other smaller fractures that might be associated with such an accident, and the left kneecap is completely detached.

The CT scan has given us fascinating new information to study, but there are still many puzzles. The theory of murder by a blow to the head has been set to rest, but the CT scan cannot tell us whether or not he was poisoned. The mystery continues.

A hush descends as Dr. Zahi Hawass and members of his Egyptian team unveil the mummy of Tutankhamun.

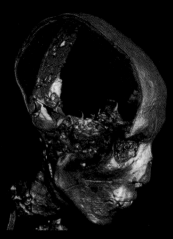

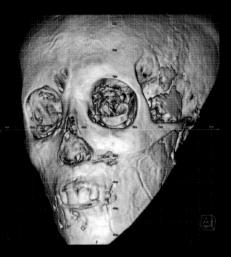

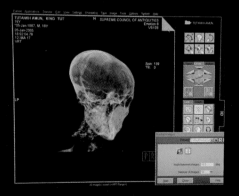

Dr. Zahi Hawass (right) helps prepare the mummy for its historic CT scan. Although Tutankhamun bore a scar on his cheek (above), three-dimensional images of the skull (left and above left) show no signs of trauma, debunking the theory that the king was murdered by a blow to the head. In the image above left, a white shadow indicates a loose fragment of bone discovered in the 1968 X-rays.

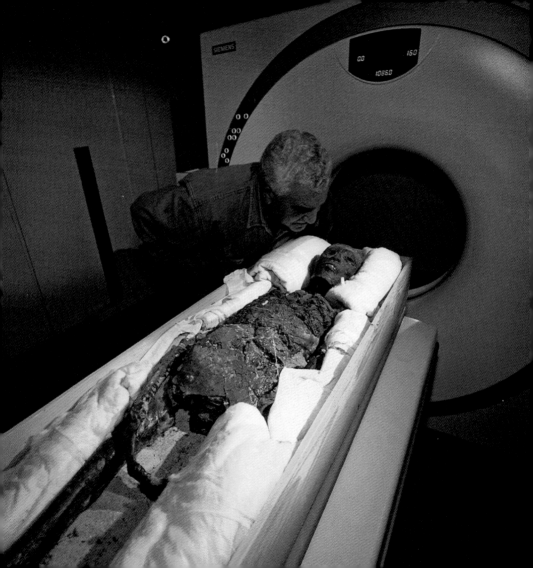

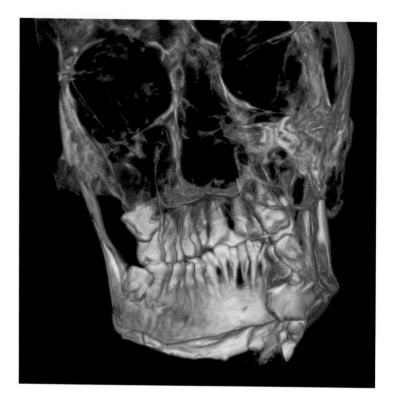

ABOVE: Head scans show that Tutankhamun had an impacted right wisdom tooth.

OPPOSITE: A 3-D reconstruction of Tutankhamun's skull, from the 2005 CT scan, shows the skull sutures.

Full-body CT scans reveal that the sternum and much of the front rib cage is missing, and indicate that the curved spine (below) is probably not a sign of disease but reflects the way the embalmers laid the king out.

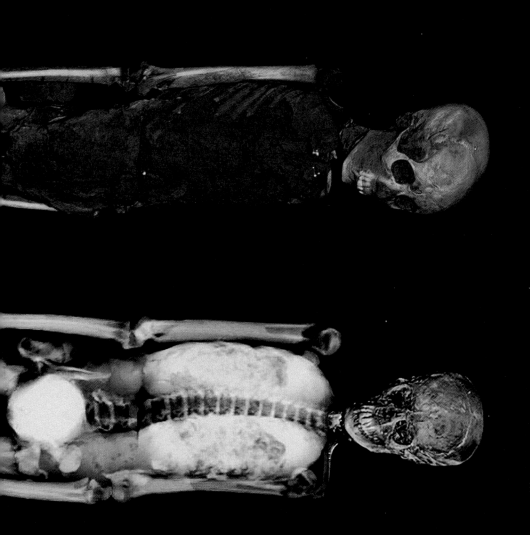

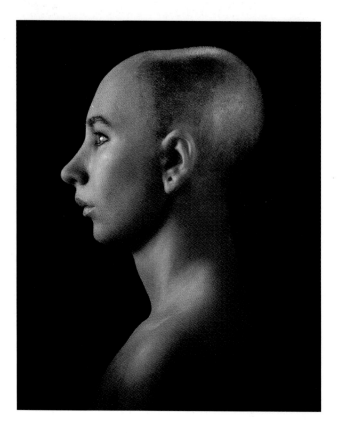

ABOVE: A reconstruction of Tutankhamun's head highlights the elongated skull characteristic of his family and the overbite seen in the mummies of his ancestors.

OPPOSITE: This latex model, a miracle of forensics based on the dimensions of Tutankhumun's skull, brings an ancient king to life.

Published by the National Geographic Society
John M. Fahey, Jr., *President and Chief Executive Officer*
Gilbert M. Grosvenor, *Chairman of the Board*
Nina D. Hoffman, *Executive Vice President*

Prepared by the Book Division
Kevin Mulroy, *Senior Vice President and Publisher*
Kristin Hanneman, *Illustrations Director*
Marianne R. Koszorus, *Design Director*

Staff for this Book
Lisa Lytton, *Project Editor*
Janice Kamrin, *Contributing Editor*
Patricia Daniels, *Text Editor*
Margo Browning, *Text Editor*
Laura Lindgren, *Art Director*
Jane Menyawi, *Illustrations Editor*
Rachel Sweeney, *Illustrations Specialist*
Dana Chivvis, *Illustrations Assistant*
Carl Mehler, *Director of Maps*
Joseph F. Ochlak, *Map Research and Edit*
Nicholas P. Rosenbach, *Map Research and Edit*
Gregory Ugiansky, *Map Production*
Tibor G. Tóth, *Map Relief*
Gary Colbert, *Production Director*
Lewis Bassford, *Production Project Manager*

Manufacturing and Quality Control
Christopher A. Liedel, *Chief Financial Officer*
Phillip L. Schlosser, *Managing Director*
John T. Dunn, *Technical Director*
Clifton M. Brown, *Manager*

**Exhibition organized by National Geographic,
Arts and Exhibitions International, and AEG Exhibitions
in association with the Supreme Council of Antiquities, Cairo**

Special Thanks to NATIONAL GEOGRAPHIC staff:
Chris Johns, Editor; Chris Sloan, Senior Editor, Art;
Chris Klein, Art Director; John Echave, Senior Editor,
Research Grant Projects; Laura Lakeway, Illustrations
Specialist; and Elizabeth Snodgrass, Researcher.

Illustration Credits
All photographs by Kenneth Garrett except the following:
Pages 2, 24: Photographs copyright © 2005 Griffith Institute,
Oxford. Page 29: Artwork courtesy of Damnfx. Pages 56, top
left and right; 58, 59, 60, 61: Digital composite and coloration by
NGM Art. Back cover, pages 62, 63: Tutankhamun reconstruction by Elisabeth Daynes; Photograph by Kenneth Garrett. CT
scanning equipment provided by Siemens AG; data courtesy of
the Supreme Council of Antiquities, Arab Republic of Egypt.

Library of Congress Cataloging-in-Publication Data available
upon request. ISBN 0-7922-5287-X (AEG)
ISBN 0-7922-5311-6 (National Geographic Books)

Published by the National Geographic Society,
45 17th Street N.W., Washington, D.C. 20036

Printed in the United States